Perfect Patterns

Written by Claire Owen

South Africa

My name is Kelsey. I live in
Johannesburg, South Africa.
There are many interesting
patterns in South Africa.
What patterns can you find
in this book?

Contents

Wherever you see me, you'll find activities to try and questions to answer.

Dazzling Designs

People in Africa have used patterns and designs to decorate their bodies, clothes, and homes for thousands of years. Designs and patterns are made using different shapes, colors, and objects. They can be painted, woven, or strung on a string.

design an arrangement of parts, colors, and patterns

Describe the designs and patterns you can see. What shapes can you find in the designs? Can you find any patterns of colors?

Sometimes a design or pattern has a special meaning or tells a special story. Artists around the world pass on their designs to their children, much as storytellers pass on their stories.

Beads, Beads, Beads

In April 2004, archaeologists were digging in a cave in South Africa. They found some beads that were 75,000 years old. The beads were made from seashells. Each bead had a hole for a string. Over the years, beads have been made from many materials, such as seeds, seashells, coral, ivory, bone, clay, and stone. They have been made and worn by people all around the world.

Archaeologists were excited when they found 41 ancient beads in Blombos Cave, South Africa.

archaeologist a scientist who studies things left by ancient peoples

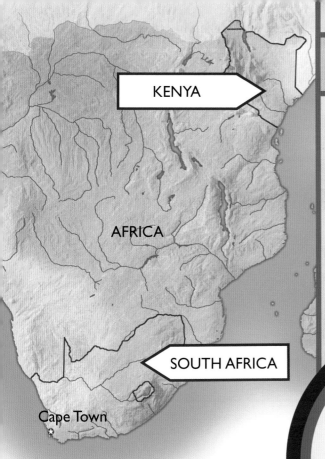

KENYA

AFRICA

SOUTH AFRICA

Cape Town

Did You Know?

Before the discovery of the seashell beads, the oldest beads ever found were about 40,000 years old. They came from Kenya, in eastern Africa, and were made from the shell of an ostrich egg.

How many years older than the Kenyan beads are the seashell beads from South Africa?

Today, glass or plastic beads are used to make colorful patterns and designs for clothes, jewelry, toys, and other objects. The Zulu, Xhosa (KO sa), and Ndebele (en DEH beh leh) peoples of South Africa are skilled bead workers.

Bead Patterns

Some necklaces of beads or seeds have a repeating pattern. We can use letters to show how the pattern repeats. For example, this necklace has two kinds of beads, *A* and *B*.

The pattern begins *ABB*. Then the same beads are repeated several times.

Another way to help show a pattern is to draw lines between the "repeats." This row of Zulu dolls also shows an *ABB* pattern.

Figure It Out

1. Use linking cubes, links, counters, or beads in two colors (A and B). Make a repeating pattern that goes—

   a. AB, AB, AB, ...

   b. AAB, AAB, AAB, ...

   c. ABBB, ABBB, ABBB, ...

2. Look at the bead necklaces U through Y.

   a. Which necklace has an ABBB pattern?

   b. Which two necklaces each have a pattern that goes ABCB, ABCB, ABCB?

   c. Use letters to describe the patterns in the other necklaces.

3. Four different kinds of beads were used to make necklace Z. Use the letters A, B, C, and D to show the pattern.

U

V

W

X

Y

Z

Simple Symmetry

The Ndebele people of South Africa create dazzling designs to decorate their homes and the clothes that they wear on special occasions.

Many museums and art galleries around the world also display examples of Ndebele art. Ndebele designs are often symmetrical.

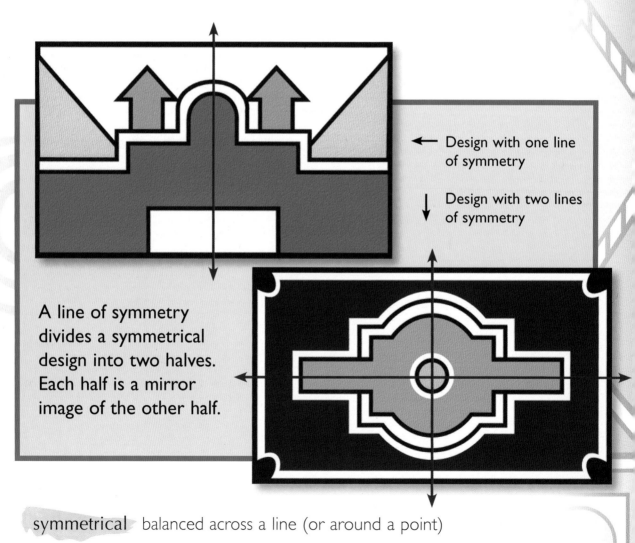

← Design with one line of symmetry

↓ Design with two lines of symmetry

A line of symmetry divides a symmetrical design into two halves. Each half is a mirror image of the other half.

symmetrical balanced across a line (or around a point)

Each rectangle on the Ndebele house (above) has a colorful design. Which designs have two lines of symmetry? Can you see any designs that are not symmetrical?

Are these Ndebele aprons symmetrical? What shapes can you see? Can you find a triangle?
... a rectangle?
... a trapezoid?

Love Letters

The colors and shapes in Zulu beadwork can have special meanings. Red, for example, can mean love, while black can mean marriage.

A young Zulu woman might make her sweetheart a beaded neckband called an *ibheqe*. This is sometimes called a "love letter," because the colors spell out a message.

Many Zulu love letters are symmetrical. The designs on some love letters have two lines of symmetry.

Make a Symmetrical Design

You will need a sheet of grid paper with half-inch or one-centimeter squares.

---

1. Fold a sheet of grid paper in half.

2. Color a design on the grid. (You could draw half of a Zulu love-letter design.)

---

3. Unfold the grid paper.

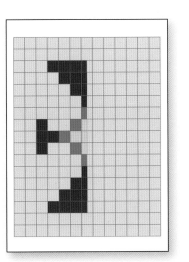

4. Color the mirror image of your design on the blank half of the grid.

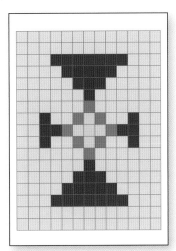

Beautiful Beadwork

Beads have been traded around the world for centuries. In some places, beads have even been used as money. From Africa to the Americas, from Italy to India, people have worn beaded clothing and jewelry. Many traditional beadwork patterns and designs are still used today.

Native American peoples used beads to decorate many things, from clothing and moccasins to harnesses for their horses.

tradition   an old and special way of doing things

The Huichol Indians of Mexico use beads to create beautiful designs on carved wooden objects.

↓

The Italian city of Venice is famous for its glasswork. In the late 1400s, craftspeople in Venice produced beautiful glass beads that were sometimes used as money in Africa.

↑

This necklace made from shell and bone is over 5,000 years old. It was found in Palestine, in the Middle East.

These boots from Nigeria, Africa, are decorated with beads.

←

Sample Answers

Page 5   Answers might include triangles, rectangles, squares, and parallelograms on the beaded belt; patterns of colors such as blue, white, blue, white on the bead headdress; and so on.

Page 7   35,000 years

Page 9
2. a. W   b. U and X
     c. V: ABACCC Y: ABBAC

3. ABACADAC (where A is a small, round, black bead)

> **Make some repeating patterns using beads, cubes, links, or counters in three or four different colors.**

Index